Asset Management (AM)

Unique and Hard-to-Value Assets

August 2012

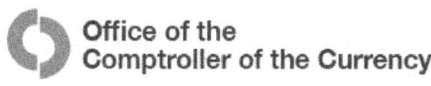

**Office of the
Comptroller of the Currency**

Washington, DC 20219

Unique and Hard-to-Value Assets

Contents

Unique and Hard-to-Value Assets   Overview

This booklet describes unique assets and hard-to-value assets, risks associated with investing or holding these assets, and the fiduciary role in managing these assets. This booklet provides guidance for examining these types of discretionary assets held in fiduciary accounts in asset management areas of national banks and federal savings associations (collectively, banks). In many instances, the guidance is equally applicable to assets held in custody accounts and to non-managed trust accounts. The guidance provides bank examiners with expanded examination procedures, which supplement the core assessment standards in the "Large Bank Supervision" and "Community Bank Supervision" booklets of the *Comptroller's Handbook*. The examination procedures are optional but may be used when a bank has a significant number of unique assets to manage or has hard-to-value assets for reporting purposes.

What Are Unique and Hard-to-Value Assets?

Unique assets include real estate, closely held businesses, mineral interests, loans and notes, life insurance, tangible assets, and collectibles. Fiduciaries generally accept these assets into trust accounts to accommodate a client's entire portfolio of assets. The most common example of this arrangement is a bank placing the family home or property into a trust. On rare occasions, a bank may *purchase* these types of assets but only if the bank has the appropriate expertise and only in accounts of significant size and sophistication.

Unique assets may also be used as investments, such as an income-producing shopping center or rental property. Management of unique assets presents numerous challenges. Real estate presents possible environmental liability. Leases for real estate—including farm, ranchland, and mineral interests—must be negotiated and rent must be collected. Collectibles must be protected and insured. Across all of these asset types, one of the common challenges is that unique characteristics make these asset types hard to value. The unique assets described in this booklet are not traded on a financial market and therefore do not have readily determined values. In contrast, other investments typically held in a trust or retirement account, such as equities and bonds, have values that are readily ascertained. In contrast with the fungibility of most securities, the specific attributes of a unique asset can affect not only its value but its marketability.

Depending on the type of unique asset held in a fiduciary or custody account, a variety of laws apply. These laws not only govern how these assets are to be monitored and administered by a fiduciary, but they also can affect how the assets are valued. Banks acting in a fiduciary capacity must invest fiduciary funds in a manner consistent with applicable law, pursuant to 12 CFR 9.11 and 12 CFR 150.260(a)[1]. Banks also must be aware of the various state laws that regulate real property ownership as well as registration requirements imposed on closely held companies. There are additional restrictions in the Internal Revenue Code for individual retirement accounts and for employee benefit plans subject to the Employee Retirement Income Securities Act (ERISA). In addition, consumer compliance laws may apply to certain loans, such as real estate mortgages, held in fiduciary accounts. Most banks do not actively buy and sell this type of asset. They are usually received in-kind or deposited during the life of the accounts. No matter how these assets are received by banks, proper administration and operational controls are critical.

Risks Associated With Unique and Hard-to-Value Assets

Asset management risks are inherent in individually managed portfolios, but the inclusion of unique assets further increases a bank's risk. Risk increases because these assets often require special expertise to manage, are sometimes subject to special ownership rules, and are frequently hard to value. Some assets present liability concerns that may extend the risk of loss beyond the amount invested. A bank fiduciary may face liability from secondary beneficiaries when holding a nonproductive asset, such as property occupied by a primary beneficiary. Other beneficiaries might question why the property was not made more productive. A bank's failure to properly manage unique assets prudently and legally can increase the bank's risks, particularly its operational, compliance, reputation, and strategic risks. This in turn may adversely affect the bank's earnings and capital.

---

[1] OCC is conducting a comprehensive review of regulations as part of the Office of Thrift Supervision's integration into the OCC. Check references mentioned in this booklet to determine the current applicability to national banks (12 CFR 9) and federal savings associations (12 CFR 150).

Operational Risk

Operational risk is the risk to current or anticipated earnings or capital arising from inadequate or failed internal processes or systems, the misconduct or errors of people, and adverse external events. This risk manifests itself in several ways. First, safeguarding unique assets owned by an account for which the bank is a fiduciary or custodian poses unique risks. This involves the physical upkeep and securing of the asset as well as maintaining the account's legal ownership of the asset. Real estate or collectibles are in this asset type. Secondly, a bank fiduciary holding unique assets such as mineral interests, real estate, or interests in closely held companies generally requires specialized accounting and control systems. Without these systems, the bank risks not properly monitoring and accounting for the various income streams and related taxes associated with these assets.

Another risk unique to this type of asset is proper transaction processing. Income-producing real estate, for example, typically has recurring transactions, such as lease payments, that are received by the bank as individual payments via checks, automated clearing house (ACH) payments, or wire transfers. The bank must process and accurately account for upkeep expenses, taxes, and insurance. Banks that do not have processing systems for these types of assets need to process these transactions manually, creating a greater likelihood of human error.

Mineral interests are another unique asset type with specialized and complex processing requirements. Mineral-interest payments from producers of oil or gas wells owned by multiple accounts are usually received in one combined check. The bank must then compute and credit each account with its fractional-share income. Mineral-interest processing typically requires specialized accounting and management reporting systems. These systems provide mechanisms for reporting and properly supervising such assets.

A bank fiduciary must ensure it has appropriate personnel in place to supervise these assets. The bank must have staff that monitors controls that track the cost of capital investments and the expenses associated with these investments. This process should be used to monitor maintenance costs as well as any improvements made to the assets.

Compliance Risk

Compliance risk is the current and prospective risk to earnings and capital arising from a violation of, or noncompliance with, laws, rules, and regulations. In the asset management business lines, compliance risk encompasses not only regulatory compliance but also compliance with applicable law and governing instruments. For example, farm and ranch real estate, as well as many mineral interests, are affected by environmental laws that subject fiduciaries to significant fines in the event of noncompliance. There can also be provisions in the governing instrument that mandate retention of an asset or restrict sales, such as the right of first refusal by beneficiaries. If the bank sells the asset without following the protocol established in the governing instrument, the bank will have violated its fiduciary duty. A bank fiduciary also needs to adhere to prudent ethical standards that require them to act in the best interests of beneficiaries. The bank fiduciary must ensure that it follows sound fiduciary principles when administering unique assets.

Asset management accounts and transactions present Bank Secrecy Act/Anti-Money Laundering (BSA/AML) and Office of Foreign Asset Control (OFAC) concerns similar to those of deposit taking, lending, and other traditional bank activities. A bank fiduciary must have sound BSA/AML and OFAC policies and procedures to comply with its obligations and must be aware of how far-reaching due diligence in this area should extend. For example, a trust may hold an entity, such as a grocery store with a money-service business as part of the operation, or an import-export business as a closely held business.

A bank fiduciary can expose itself to compliance risk if it fails to adhere to the bank's policies and procedures or fails to secure needed expertise. For instance, if a bank fiduciary invests in or accepts an asset that is not authorized or even prohibited by bank policy, the fiduciary can be criticized for failing to comply with bank policy. The bank fiduciary that lacks expertise in managing a particular asset type, such as certain mineral interests, may choose to delegate the management of those assets. The bank fiduciary should still have sufficient understanding of the underlying risks and characteristics presented by those assets to properly supervise outside managers of those assets.

Strategic Risk

A bank fiduciary assumes strategic risk when taking on new product lines without having the expertise and systems to properly manage and control risks associated with the line of business. The risk level depends on the compatibility of an organization's strategic goals and the business strategies developed to achieve these goals. Because the management of unique assets falls outside the more traditional equity and fixed-income strategies, management must ensure that personnel are qualified to manage these assets. With more traditional financial investments, administrators have numerous financial tools to monitor performance and do not need to focus on physical safekeeping of the assets. Because unique asset market values are associated with a specific asset, financial reviews have to be tailored to the particular asset and its real or potential profitability.

Reputation Risk

The manner in which a bank fiduciary manages unique assets on behalf of its fiduciary customers may have a significant impact on the bank's reputation. A bank fiduciary's lack of expertise or oversight of unique assets can subject the bank to significant losses, potential litigation, and reputation risk. Bank fiduciaries must ensure that they have sufficient processes and resources in place to manage, secure, and protect unique assets under their care. Tangible assets and collectibles can present heightened reputation risk. Beneficiaries often have a sentimental attachment to such items and it may not be possible to replace them if they are lost or damaged.

Reputation risk may arise if a bank does not have the expertise to administer an asset type, monitor the condition of the asset, or assess a value for those assets, and the bank is ultimately required to outsource those processes. Because third-party providers act as agent for the bank, any weakness in third-party supervision has the potential to affect the bank directly through negative publicity or litigation. Because many fiduciary relationships result from client referrals, maintaining a good reputation is critical to building future business.

Risk Mitigation–Unique and Hard-to-Value Assets

Risk Management

The specialized expertise needed to manage, analyze, and value unique assets makes sound risk management processes essential. Because risk strategies and organizational structures vary, there is no standardized risk management system that works for every bank. Each bank should establish comprehensive risk management systems based on its size and complexity to ensure that the system is suited to each bank's needs and circumstances. When developing its risk management structure, a bank should consider the size and complexity of the unique assets invested and managed by the bank fiduciary. The "Asset Management" booklet of the *Comptroller's Handbook* provides additional guidance on risk management systems for all asset types.

Risk Supervision

The bank's board of directors and senior management should take appropriate steps to identify, measure, control, and monitor the risks associated with investing and managing unique assets. The bank fiduciary has a duty to maintain and protect the value of a trust's assets and to make them productive. Board and management must commit to and support comprehensive risk management systems that effectively manage risk associated with unique assets. These systems should include specific processes for each class of unique assets held or managed by the bank's trust department, including

- a review of each asset annually (not necessarily at the same time for each asset or asset class) in conjunction with a review of the account's more readily marketable financial assets.

- policy guidelines for valuation frequency and methods.

- sufficient expertise to monitor any third party managing these assets. This oversight is particularly critical when unique assets such as real estate, oil, gas, or mining interests are held in a fiduciary account.

- processes to provide appropriate insurance coverage and ensure relevant taxes are paid.

- a process to ensure and track timely management actions and documentation, particularly in terms of sale decisions.

- a process to track income from unique assets and to ensure payments are received and appropriate action is taken when not received in a timely manner.

- controls, such as audit and compliance reviews, to ensure the bank follows its policies and procedures appropriately.

Risk Assessment

A risk assessment helps the bank identify its risks, determine how to measure those risks, and assess the quality of the controls and monitoring systems. The bank's risk assessment should address the changing risk characteristics and expectations of the bank's client portfolio, including identifying applicable risks posed by the assets held in those accounts. Management should focus on the following items when developing its risk assessment:

- Types and volume of unique assets managed in the bank; and the types of accounts holding those assets;

- Expertise needed to manage the volume and complexity of unique assets;

- Sources of information and methodology used to value these assets;

- Adequacy of systems to handle the volume of assets, the valuation of the various types of assets, and the bank's ability to provide timely management reports that document the volume, value, and performance of these assets both individually and collectively;

- Adequacy of audit and compliance oversight and testing, including BSA/AML and OFAC; and

- Adequate documentation, event tracking, and exception reporting systems and mechanisms.

Risk Controls

Risk controls are policies, procedures, processes, and systems that help control and mitigate risk. The types, breadth, and depth of controls should be consistent with the board's risk tolerance. Risk controls include

- Risk tolerance for the volume and types of unique assets the bank invests in or manages. These standards should include correlating the size of the real estate portfolio to the trust department staff's capabilities and limiting the geographic footprint of real estate or mineral interests to a size or scope that can be effectively monitored.

- A monitoring process for tracking and reporting exceptions to ensure that follow up and corrective action is completed.

- Adequate internal control processes to safeguard unique assets. This is particularly important with such tangible assets as collectibles or art work that can be stolen and with security documents for closely held companies that can be misplaced. Controls should take into account the fact that collectibles and artwork are not always secured by the bank. They are often left in the residence of a surviving spouse or other beneficiary who may be a co-owner with the trust account.

- Proper separation of duties both within and among administration and operational areas. For example, areas such as receipt of income and payment of expenses require separation to ensure proper controls and accountability.

Other key risk controls over unique assets include the account review processes mandated by 12 CFR 9.6 and 12 CFR 150.200-220.

Pre-acceptance review–12 CFR 9.6(a) and 12 CFR 150.200: Before accepting a fiduciary account, a bank shall review the prospective account to determine whether the trust department has the resources and expertise to administer the account properly.

The pre-acceptance review is the key assessment used to identify the type of assets in each account the department is ultimately responsible for administering. This preliminary review process may be used to screen out types of unique assets that the bank has determined it does not want—or does not have the resources—to manage or that pose heightened litigation or reputation risks exceeding the bank's risk appetite. A bank may also decide that certain asset types are too costly to manage and cannot be profitably held in a fiduciary account.

Management should have a well-defined process for evaluating and inspecting real estate and mineral interests before acceptance. Management should use experts who understand these assets and who provide a level of consistency when evaluating these assets. During this review, the bank or its experts should determine whether the bank has sufficient expertise to manage the unique assets, determine whether potential environmental concerns and liability have been addressed adequately, and ensure systems, operations, and administrative personnel have the resources to properly administer these assets.

During this process, the fiduciary should evaluate its responsibilities under the governing instrument, local law, and grantor and beneficiary expectations. In the case of real estate, mineral interests, and closely held businesses, the bank should pay particular attention to the location of the assets, as it may be more costly and difficult to manage assets located out-of-territory, in other states, or abroad. Because some states limit ownership of real estate to resident bank fiduciaries, a nonresident fiduciary may need to hire an ancillary bank fiduciary to hold title to out-of-state real estate. The fee charged for managing assets in other states should reflect the heightened risk, legal expenses, and other additional costs that the fiduciary is accepting. Another factor to consider is the degree and type of ownership. A bank with a majority interest in a closely held business has a great deal more responsibility than a minority owner. Limited partners have limited liability while general partners do not, and working mineral interests present greater potential liability than royalty interests.

Management should thoroughly inspect any property that potentially has environmental issues and should perform due diligence to determine local regulatory requirements and constraints, particularly in unfamiliar jurisdictions. Examples include: real property owned by the trust; leasehold interests in real estate; collateral assignments on real estate mortgages; interests in partnerships, or closely held businesses that own real property.

There are three phases of environmental inspections. Phase 1 is a visual inspection. Phase 2 involves testing for contamination. Phase 3 is an actual cleanup. The reader can find a description of phase 1, 2, and 3 inspections in appendix B of this booklet. The U.S. Environmental Protection Agency (EPA) provides additional information about fiduciary liability and Superfund sites on www.epa.gov.

Bank trust department policies should set clear guidelines for the level of environmental due diligence that must be performed by the bank *before* accepting real estate, mineral interests, or closely held businesses as trust assets or accepting an appointment to administer an estate that holds such assets. Environmental liability can attach itself as soon as the bank comes into the chain of title and may even exist after the bank's involvement with the asset ends. In the unlikely event that the bank decides to accept an asset with environmental issues, the bank must ensure there is a plan in place to resolve those issues.

A common practice to mitigate a bank fiduciary's risk is to require the governing instrument to contain indemnification language to keep an asset. Letters of direction from the power-holder for property a client wishes the bank to retain, such as beneficiary-occupied real estate, are also appropriate. However, these letters of direction (also known as retention letters) should be updated periodically to ensure they remain the wishes of the client.

Initial post-acceptance review–12 CFR 9.6(b) and 12 CFR 150.210: Upon acceptance of a fiduciary account for which a bank has investment discretion, the bank shall conduct a *prompt review* (approximately 60 days after substantial funding of the account) to evaluate all assets of the account to ensure they are appropriate.

By the time of the initial post-acceptance review, the bank should have evaluated the needs of the grantor and beneficiaries and established investment objectives. This review is designed to ensure that all assets for which the bank has investment discretion meet the objectives of the account or that action plans have been established for disposition of the asset. It is also an opportunity to ensure that all assets have been properly received and titled by the bank. This review must incorporate any discretionary unique assets and must assess how these assets fit into the account's overall investment goals. This review provides management with the opportunity to make decisions regarding the selection of an outside manager, if needed, to directly manage these assets. The trust department should also obtain the most current market values for these assets to ensure the bank has the most accurate values on its books. Appropriate documentation to properly manage these assets should be in place, including the following:

- Each asset should be properly titled. Title insurance should be obtained for real estate. If required under state law, title insurance must be properly registered.

- The status of property taxes and insurance coverage should be determined and documented.

- If outside managers are to be used to manage an asset, the bank needs to enter into comprehensive and properly executed agreements with those managers.

- As determined by the pre-acceptance review, documented plans of action to address existing environmental issues must be formalized and must include time frames for correction.

- If physical assets, such as collectibles, art, or personal effects, are being held off premises, evidence is required that they are appropriately housed and are properly secured.

Annual review–12 CFR 9.6(c) and 12 CFR 150.220: At least *once during every calendar year*, a bank shall conduct a review of all assets of each fiduciary account for which the bank has investment discretion to evaluate whether the assets are appropriate, individually and collectively, for the account.

On an annual basis, each unique asset for which the bank has investment discretion must be reviewed to determine whether the asset remains an appropriate holding for the account's portfolio. The review should evaluate how these assets are made productive (either as income-producing or appreciating assets), unless otherwise authorized by the governing instrument. For income-producing unique assets, the review should contain financial analysis demonstrating performance. The bank fiduciary should compare the unique asset's performance with other similar assets and other potential investments. OCC Bulletin 2008-10, "Fiduciary Activities of National Banks: Annual Reviews of Fiduciary Accounts Pursuant to 12 CFR 9.6(c)," and 12 CFR 150–220 outline the type of information expected in these reviews. The review should also consider actual income generated, passive income and expense management for tax purposes, and the tax consequences of selling the assets. If bank staff does not have the expertise to provide this information, the bank must retain vendors with appropriate expertise to perform this analysis. The annual review should ensure valuations are appropriate, inspections have been addressed, and taxes and insurance are current.

Risk Monitoring

Management should have policies and procedures in place that ensure compliance with laws, rules, regulations, and sound fiduciary practices. This is particularly important with real estate because state and local laws and regulations govern real property. Monitoring processes should be in place to ensure that high-risk properties are properly administered, procedures are implemented to mitigate risk, responsibilities are assigned for correction, and time frames are set for corrective actions. In addition, a bank should have mechanisms in place to elevate higher-risk assets to the attention of senior management and to monitor accounts and transactions for suspicious activity.

Personnel and Department Organization

Supervision of unique and hard-to-value assets should be organized to match the volume, risk, and complexity of the property held. A small bank trust department, whose accounts hold only non-complex unique assets, may require that account administrators manage the property held in these trusts. Departments with more complex real estate holdings may find it more appropriate to form a committee to manage real estate. Committee members typically include trust department management, representatives from the bank's credit department, and outside board members with real estate expertise.

When unique asset holdings are significant or complex, many trust departments establish separate departments to supervise these different types of holdings. Personnel in these functional areas should have specialized knowledge and experience. Their duties may range from managing farm and ranch properties (and the commodities produced on those properties) to managing timber interests, leasing commercial buildings, or, in limited cases, purchasing real estate investment holdings.

Some bank trust departments find it more effective to outsource property management instead of hiring full-time professionals. Any vendor the bank engages to manage property should have experience managing similar properties. Depending on the volume and complexity of the asset involved, the bank fiduciary may engage part-time or full-time third-party managers.

The bank fiduciary should only delegate duties pursuant to a written management agreement prepared by legal counsel. The agreement should specify each party's responsibilities to ensure the bank fiduciary retains control over remittances, such as lease payments and expenditures, repairs, and maintenance. Any management agreement should address insurance bonding in the event of wrongdoing by the asset manager. The agreement should include language that ensures that the third-party manager provides to the bank the information the bank needs to effectively oversee the property manager's work. For vendors or agents who provide material services to the bank, refer to OCC Bulletin 2001-47, "Third-Party Relationships: Risk Management Principles" for guidance. As indicated in this bulletin, "no single system is ideal for every bank. Large banks typically require sophisticated risk management systems involving a complex and diverse array of third-party products and services. On the other hand, community banks may be able to comply with this guidance in a less formal and systematic manner because of the relative simplicity of their risk exposures and management's direct knowledge of the third parties."

Types of Unique and Hard-to-Value Assets

Real Estate

Real estate assets can represent significant holdings in fiduciary accounts. These holdings may include any of the major realty types: residential, retail, office, agricultural, industrial, and vacant land. Historically, it would be unusual for a bank fiduciary to purchase an individual parcel of real estate. Such purchases are usually limited to residences or family-oriented farms or ranches. Real estate is generally received in-kind at the account's inception or is subsequently transferred by the grantor out of his or her name and into the trust.

Bank fiduciaries are responsible for properly managing all types of real property. They must have in-depth knowledge of prudent real property management, including market knowledge, accounting and legal expertise, diversification of holdings where possible, and careful oversight and monitoring of each asset. Property held for investment and potential sale requires different skills and management techniques than property, such as a residence, held for the use of a beneficiary. If the real estate does not produce income for the trust, the bank fiduciary must determine whether retaining the property is in the best interests of the trust.

Bank fiduciaries must ensure that property is maintained and made productive, while attempting to maximize the return for the account. They must take timely action through appropriate management tools. For example, tickler systems remind management to collect rent, manage leases, update insurance, perform inspections, obtain environmental evaluations, and pay taxes on time. Checklists guide administrators through the steps to ensure that these tasks are performed. Exceptions to established processes should be reported to the board or a designated committee, and a tracking system should be maintained to follow up on missing documentation or deficiencies. A bank trust department that invests in and manages a large number of real estate properties may operate at the direction of a real estate committee that oversees these activities.

A bank fiduciary should have current information about the condition and the value of each property. This information is needed to make risk assessments and property management decisions. The real estate file should contain documentation supporting the bank fiduciary's actions. The level of documentation needed depends on the complexity and risks associated with each holding and the applicable laws governing the property. Required documentation includes evidence of ownership, valuations and inspections, insurance, environmental reviews, leases, and payment of taxes. The file should document how the property is being maintained. See appendix C of this booklet for an optional worksheet for reviewing a real estate sample.

Evidence of Ownership

If a bank owns real estate as part of a fiduciary relationship, the bank trust department must have evidence of ownership by a specific trust. "Title" is used in the context of legal "possession" of the property. The terms "good title" and "clear title" refer to a title that is free of litigation risks, liens, and defects. Before purchasing real estate, a prudent fiduciary must consider whether the current owner is able to pass clear title. Two methods for assuring that clear title can be conveyed are (1) a legal search is performed and an opinion is provided; and (2) a formal title search is performed and title insurance is obtained.

Land ownership is documented with a deed. The most common forms of deeds are warranty, quitclaim, and executor's deed.

A warranty deed indicates that the grantor or owner possesses the title free and clear of imperfections. The transfer under this form of deed creates a liability on the part of the grantor/owner of the property, and is subject to recourse by the purchaser if defects exist.

A quitclaim deed merely conveys whatever title the grantor/owner has or claims to have in the property. No recourse exists against the grantor. In fact, a grantor/owner signing a quitclaim deed may have no legal title to the property at all.

The executor of an estate conveys **an executor deed** as part of a sale or distribution. While the OCC does not require a particular title search method or type of deed, it is important that the bank fiduciary have an effective process in place to minimize future litigation. It is a bank fiduciary's basic duty to gather assets and, as part of this process, to take reasonable steps to ensure the trust has clear title to the property.

Inspections

Inspections should be performed on at least an annual basis in conjunction with the account's annual investment review, as required by 12 CFR 9.6(c) and 12 CFR 150.220 and OCC Bulletin 2008-10, "Fiduciary Activities of National Banks: Annual Reviews of Fiduciary Accounts Pursuant to 12 CFR 9.6(c)." Inspections are required for all real estate properties and mineral working interests when the bank has investment discretion. The purpose of the inspection is to keep the bank fiduciary informed of the condition of the property. The trust department's policy for holding real estate should provide guidelines for the timing and contents of inspections. Some items to consider include

- the economic condition of the neighborhood.

- any deterioration in the structure.

- lease maturities and tenant quality.

- any conditions that could lead to liability hazards or risks.

- any known contamination or environmental problems.

- the date of previous inspection/appraisal.

- the current status of tax and insurance payments on the property.

In limited situations, inspections may be waived by the grantor or other individual who has authority over the account. If dealing with a co-trustee, or grantor with diminished capacity, the bank must ensure waiving inspections is a safe and sound practice and appropriate for the property. If an inspection is waived, the fiduciary should document the reasons for doing so. If owner/grantors or beneficiaries occupy the property, if the owner/grantor is on-site on an ongoing basis, or if the trust only owns a fractional interest in the property, a less detailed inspection may be appropriate. It remains the bank fiduciary's duty to ensure the property is being maintained properly through an appropriate level of inspection.

Environmental Issues

Environmental issues are a source of potentially significant risk to fiduciaries managing real property. Since the enactment of the Comprehensive Environmental Response, Compensation, and Liability Act of 1980 (CERCLA) (also known as the Superfund Act) and the Superfund Amendments and Reauthorization Act of 1986 (SARA), environmental liability has become a critical issue for bank fiduciaries. CERCLA allows for recovery of cleanup costs by the EPA. Cleanup costs can be material and may have a significant impact on returns on investment. In 1997, the Asset Conservation, Lender Liability, and Deposit Insurance Protection Act of 1996 (ACA) amended CERCLA to clarify and, under defined circumstances, limit a fiduciary's liability. The ACA provided "safe harbor activities for fiduciaries to take, or decline to take, without incurring personal liability when managing property in a trust." These activities are particularly critical if land or properties that may have housed hazardous materials are taken into a trust.

Under CERCLA Section 107(n), fiduciary liability under any provision of CERCLA cannot exceed assets held in the fiduciary capacity. In addition, a fiduciary may not be found liable in its personal capacity for certain actions, such as

- undertaking or requiring another person to undertake any lawful means of addressing a release of a hazardous substance.

- enforcing environmental compliance terms of the fiduciary agreement.

- administering a facility that was contaminated before the fiduciary relationship began.

Under the ACA, however, *a fiduciary is considered personally responsible for cleaning up a property if its negligence contributed to the site's contamination.* EPA designed these criteria to prevent fiduciary relationships from being established to avoid cleanup costs.

For mineral interest assets, the potential for environmental liability depends on the type of mineral interest held. This is discussed in more detail in the "Mineral Interests" section of this booklet.

Valuations

Asset valuation is a critical component when determining whether a bank fiduciary should retain a property. As part of the 12 CFR 9.6(c) and 12 CFR 150.220 annual investment review, the bank fiduciary must make a determination for accounts in which the bank has investment discretion whether to retain a property or sell it and whether to reinvest the funds in another asset. One of the factors used to make these decisions is the assessment of the property's value. Valuations are also used to initially determine and thereafter maintain the appropriate level of insurance required on improved real estate.

Accurate asset valuations are critical. Asset valuations determine the position and market values reported on client statements and on online client reporting systems. These valuations are used to determine the appropriate level of insurance required for each tangible or real estate asset, and they are used for regulatory reports (for example, Schedule RC-T "Fiduciary and Related Services" of the Consolidated Report of Condition and Income). In many cases, the bank's administration fee is based on the market value of the account. Depending on the type of account, the market value—as reflected on the asset management accounting system—may be reportable in certain Internal Revenue Service (IRS) filings; may determine the amount of distributions made to beneficiaries; and may be used by clients to prepare financial reports, including audited financial statements subject to generally accepted accounting principles (GAAP). See page 29 of the "Asset Management Operations and Controls" booklet of the *Comptroller's Handbook.*

For investments, such as real estate, also closely held businesses, and mineral interests, that may not be readily priced, it may be difficult to obtain regular or reliable valuations. Methods of valuing these investments include appraisals, theoretical financial models, and bank personnel and unique asset committee estimates. *While not required by regulation, the OCC does view the triennial real estate appraisal as a safe and sound banking practice to ensure the value of a property is accurate.* Tax assessments, while appropriate for tax authorities, should not solely be relied on for valuations unless benchmarked against other data. In fact, the bank fiduciary should evaluate the reasonableness of the tax assessed value and, where appropriate, challenge those assessments.

Valuation methods should provide detail, and their accuracy should be verifiable. Valuations should be performed as frequently as feasible and whenever a material event occurs. "Material" should be clearly defined and the primary valuation factors for these assets should be determined. Any change in the primary valuation factors or any material event should trigger a valuation update. See Portfolio and Asset Valuation section of the "Investment Management Services" booklet of the *Comptroller's Handbook* for more details.

At a minimum, independent appraisals should be obtained when a property is being sold or purchased so the bank fiduciary can adequately support the property's value. Independent appraisals must be performed annually on real estate held in employee benefit accounts to ensure accurate reporting requirements on IRS Form 5500, "Annual Return/Report of Employee Benefit Plan." For individual retirement accounts (IRA), trustees are responsible for ensuring that all IRA assets (including those not traded on established markets or with otherwise readily determinable market value, such as real estate) are valued annually at their fair market value. Because of the potential difficulty with determining valuations of hard to value or illiquid assets annually, banks should use caution when accepting these types of assets in IRA accounts.

A bank trust department may obtain real property values from bank personnel with expertise outside of the trust department, who regularly perform appraisals. If the bank's trustee fee is based on the market value of the property, however, a potential conflict of interest occurs. In those instances, the bank fiduciary should obtain valuations from an independent source.

Underlying values of leased commercial properties, such as office buildings, industrial parks, and strip malls, relate to current market lease terms. A bank should consider a current, formal, and independent appraisal before renewing a lease. A bank fiduciary needs to ensure that the lease rates are consistent with current market rates. This ensures that the asset is being made as productive as possible. Between lease renewal dates, the bank fiduciary may rely on less formal inspections and analyses of trends about the property.

Similarly, for rented residential property, bank fiduciaries need information to support decisions made regarding the appropriate terms and levels of rental rates. The value, commercial nature, and underlying type of property should guide the bank fiduciary's selection of the type of appraisal needed. A large apartment complex or substantial commercial property requires more comprehensive analysis of the property's value than smaller rental properties, such as single-family homes.

For undivided fractional interests in properties, such as when a parcel of land is owned by several individuals including a trust, several factors influence a fiduciary's decision regarding the frequency of valuations. What are the terms of the governing instrument regarding decisions about the property? Does the bank fiduciary have a controlling interest in the property, perhaps through a combination of related accounts? Are there any concerns with the grantor or beneficiaries (such as the potential for litigation between the bank fiduciary and the holders of the fractional interests)? Generally, the bank fiduciary can rely on informal inspections and analyses of trends about such property. If the clients are difficult to deal with or are litigious, however, a bank fiduciary may need to carefully and more formally support property valuation decisions.

Grantor- and beneficiary-occupied residences are examples of circumstances in which bank fiduciaries may rely on informal inspections and analyses of trends for valuations. There are numerous public and private Web sites that can facilitate determinations of informal residential real estate valuations. For example, many state and county governments provide property tax information on public Web sites that include the entity's valuation of the properties. Similarly, there are private Web sites that track recorded residential real estate sale prices. While not a substitute for an appraisal and frequently lagging marketplace changes, these sources provide a range of valuations that may be used between formal appraisals.

For information about the formal appraisal process, and the cost, markets, and income approaches to value, refer to OCC Bulletin 2010-42, "Sound Practices for Appraisals and Evaluations: Interagency Appraisal and Evaluation Guidelines." It is important to be aware that appraisals of properties held in trust are not subject to the regulations that govern appraisals for commercial loans. As fiduciary properties are not being held as collateral for a loan, their values do not need to be monitored as frequently or closely. Whether it is a commercial loan or a trust property, however, the approaches for determining values are the same, and the characteristics of a good quality appraisal are fundamentally similar.

The trust department should have board-approved policies that establish guidelines and minimum appraisal requirements. The bank's compliance systems should identify and track corrective actions for exceptions to these policies. Management should clearly document the reasons supporting a policy exception and identify whether it is a temporary or permanent exception.

Insurance

Insurance requirements vary with the type and nature of the properties. Generally, improved properties should have hazard and liability insurance, including provisions for fire, flood, theft, and natural disasters. Unimproved properties should, at a minimum, have liability coverage. Based on an analysis of costs and benefits, a fiduciary might consider other types of insurance. For example, rent interruption insurance may be prudent in order to replace rents lost because of certain events for a specified period. Also appropriate may be off-premises services coverage or utility insurance that covers the loss of rental income associated with an interruption of services caused by physical losses beyond the property itself. Boiler and machinery insurance may be appropriate for industrial properties or manufacturing plants held in trust to provide insurance coverage for lost revenues when certain equipment is under repair.

A bank trust department often purchases a master insurance policy covering most or all properties managed by the department. The bank is responsible for providing information about each property to the insurance provider on acceptance of the property. Master policies often cover replacement cost for individual properties, with an aggregate limit of loss for the bank. Many master policies also provide liability coverage. The bank should have management tools in place, such as tickler systems, to alert management to policy expiration dates and to prompt requests to obtain needed documentation. Periodic valuations coupled with insurance coverage reviews ensure that the amount of insurance coverage is adequate. Insurance is an extremely important means of transferring risk and limiting the risk of litigation.

Farm and Ranch Management

There are special considerations when crops and livestock are being raised on real property. The bank fiduciary usually is responsible not only for the underlying property of the account administered but also for the farm's or ranch's production. If the bank fiduciary leases the land, it should ensure that the tenant is capable, experienced, and knowledgeable about the particular operation. The bank fiduciary should obtain summary financial information about the income and expenses related to the farm's or ranch's production. To understand and analyze a farm's or ranch's financial information, the bank fiduciary needs to be familiar with the cycle of production for the crop or livestock. For instance, crop share leases are common for certain types of crops with related expenses (seed, fertilizer, etc.) shared proportionately. Because crop insurance varies by geography and type of crop, a bank fiduciary is responsible for ensuring the most cost-effective insurance is in place. The bank fiduciary must also evaluate the potential benefits and limitations associated with government farm programs to assess the merits of participation.

The bank fiduciary also needs detailed reports to properly monitor production progress. Periodic farm management status reports should document the type of crops planted, when harvest is expected and projected, and actual yields. Harvested crops are often stored in grain elevators or other storage facilities until sold. The bank fiduciary should verify where the commodities are held through warehouse receipts and other documents. The bank fiduciary also needs to ensure that crops are protected from spoilage or loss.

Livestock need to be inspected periodically by the bank fiduciary or by the fiduciary's agent. The inspection should give a head count of the livestock by breed, sex, and age, with a market value. The inspection should include comments on the weight and general health of the animals and veterinary expenses. The inspection should provide information specific to the type of operation, including breeding, grazing, or feedlot operations. Inspections for grazing operations should include comments on the quality of the grassland and related factors.

The use of outside agricultural managers is common, and they should be carefully vetted. These outside managers should be familiar with the types of agriculture properties being managed as well as the local agricultural economy. A manager should not be hired simply because the manager has ties to the bank or his or her property is adjacent to the trust property. The bank should have documented criteria for the selection and assessment of the manager's performance.

Agricultural managers, either in the bank's asset management department or external professionals, may recommend the use of hedging strategies to protect future selling prices. Before hedging strategies are used, the bank fiduciary should determine whether the governing instrument or applicable law authorizes such strategies. Information about financial analysis, production cycles, hedging strategies, and other guidance on sound banking practices may be found in the "Agricultural Lending" booklet of the *Comptroller's Handbook*. Also see appendix D of this Unique and Hard to Value Asset booklet for a sample worksheet when reviewing farm and ranch property.

Commercial Real Estate Leases

Commercial real estate (CRE) leases may be held as a trust investment and is typically leased to generate income. A trust that holds CRE leases may target one or more of the five primary real estate sectors: office, retail, industrial, hospitality, and residential (multifamily and one- to four-family). CRE leases are commonly received in kind or deposited into the trust by a grantor. An adequate appraisal of the property should be in place to ensure the asset is properly valued.

Leased properties should be governed by detailed, formal leases that are reviewed by legal counsel. Leases should be reviewed to ensure that protective covenants are in place and that the rights and responsibilities of both the lessor and the lessee are detailed. Rights and responsibilities that should be addressed in any lease are insurance, taxes, maintenance, time of rent payment, rent escalation clauses, easements, and inspection rights. When selecting a tenant, a fiduciary should carefully evaluate relevant factors of a lease arrangement, such as the business type, how long the tenant has been a going concern, and history with other landlords. Such factors are necessary to protect rent values and the account's investment and to guard against possible complaints or litigation. Environmental considerations are also of great importance when selecting tenants. By-products of certain operations, such as gas stations, dry cleaners, and printers, can be detrimental to property values and may subject the account and, ultimately, the fiduciary, to environmental risk. See "Environmental Issues" discussed in the "Risk Controls" section earlier in this booklet.

Timber Interests

There are special considerations when timber is held in a trust. Like other types of unique assets, timber interests are typically transferred to the bank's trust department in kind at the initiation of a trust. Less frequently, timber interests may be purchased by a bank fiduciary, primarily at the direction of the grantor.

The bank trust department's timber interest records should describe the type of trees grown and the trees' intended use. The amount of funds generated from sales depends whether the timber is intended for paper production, building materials, or furniture. The trust manager with responsibility for this area should have a written plan for timber management. The timber management plan should include the timing of tree harvestings and planting replacements.

Because the growth cycle of commercial-grade trees is 20 to 30 years, the timing of harvesting should consider favorable prices, the client's tax situation, and specific account income needs. The manager should ensure that harvesting and preparation for replanting follow timber management practices that avoid environmental damage or that negatively affect future yields. The timber management plan may include provisions that address thinning the replanted forest after 10 to 15 years, as well as other strategies designed to improve growth. A bank fiduciary should require periodic status reports from the timber property manager to monitor conformance with the plan. These timber reports detail when trees are to be cut, document bids from potential purchasers, document to whom trees are sold and at what price. The governing instrument should state how the proceeds from the sale of timber are allocated between principal and income. Additional forest income may be derived from the sale of hunting leases on the land. If hunting is allowed, the bank fiduciary should either purchase a liability policy, or require documentation of coverage from those securing hunting rights on the property.

Mineral Interests

The term "mineral interest" refers to the rights to the oil, gas, and solid minerals in a property. There are many forms of mineral interest ownership, each of which gives the holder differing rights and liabilities. Consequently, mineral interests have varying levels of risk. In most cases, bank fiduciaries do not purchase mineral interests as investments. Instead, mineral interests are usually deposited as original assets of a trust or acquired at death of the grantor or testator. Proper management of mineral interests requires personnel with highly specialized expertise, experience, and industry contacts. Many trust departments seek outside professional assistance to ensure that these assets are properly administered. Banks with income-producing mineral interests need specialized accounting and control systems to manage them.

Bank fiduciaries must ensure that processes are in place to properly manage mineral interests. The most common types of mineral interests are royalty interests and working interests.

- **Royalty interest** (RI): Interest retained by the mineral interest holder when the property is leased. The RI receives a specified portion of mineral income without any of the development and operating costs (except for certain taxes).

- **Working interest** (WI): A working interest is an interest in which the account participates (shares) with the operator of the well or mine in the actual expenses of drilling, mining, or maintaining the property. This provides the account a greater share of the income remaining after deducting all RI. That share is substantially higher than the RI but also imposes a greater share of expenses and potential liability.

When dealing with mineral interests, the bank fiduciary must utilize management tools to initiate timely action and to track documentation. For example, there should be a process to ensure timely and accurate posting of royalty and other income checks received from well and mine operators. Documentation should coincide with the terms of the lease agreements signed by the asset owner (the trust) and the operating company (the oil or mining company). This documentation should specify the percentage of interest that the trust receives from the operating company based on the mine or well's production. Based on industry practice, the minimum royalty a lessor customarily receives is 12.5 percent (one-eighth) of every dollar's worth of oil or gas produced from the lessor's property. It is common to refer to ownership interests in terms of one-eighths. Mineral interest documentation should also include the frequency that income is to be paid as well as which parties receive what percentage of income.

The bank fiduciary may be responsible for negotiating mineral leases. The bank fiduciary should consider selling working interests where the costs of administration exceed the benefits of holding the assets. A trust department should have tickler systems to remind the fiduciary to review and ensure expenses are current such as taxes and insurance coverage. A bank fiduciary should maintain documentation to support proper administration. This documentation should include evidence of ownership, valuations, leases, income and expenses, and environmental issues.

Evidence of Ownership

Several documents may be used as evidence of ownership, including the governing instrument, division orders, and mineral deeds.

- Division orders prepared by the drilling or mining company detail a land owner's rights to production payments. The division orders include the fractional or decimal percentage of ownership in the mineral interest or production, and may contain details regarding expense payments. While the bank fiduciary typically uses the division order to check the calculation of income and expense payments, the fiduciary should first ensure that the ownership percentages and production shares are accurate.

- Mineral and royalty deeds convey ownership. Mineral deeds convey title to designated minerals on or under a specific surface property, usually in perpetuity. A royalty deed conveys an interest in royalty mineral interests, often for a stipulated period.

Mineral interests received in kind or deposited as original trust assets pass ownership from the grantor to the bank fiduciary through the governing instrument. The governing instrument should authorize the bank fiduciary to hold mineral rights and should describe the bank fiduciary's management powers. If the grantor specifically relieves the bank fiduciary of liability for holding mineral interests regardless of whether those interests generate income, the governing instrument should expressly include this language. Several state laws provide this exculpatory language as well. Upon accepting mineral interests, a bank fiduciary should contact the county tax assessor where the minerals are located and file an affidavit of ownership. This affidavit assists potential investors in locating the owner of the mineral interest.

Valuations

Engineering reports typically value minerals by estimating recoverable reserves, the life of the well or mineral-bearing property, and the future price of the minerals produced. The basic value of minerals depends on the cash flow that the mineral interests generate from production. Reliance on engineering reports is the most widely accepted method for determining the valuation of mineral interests. For evaluation purposes, an independent engineering firm must prepare acceptable engineering reports, which must include detailed analyses of mineral reserves. An engineering report must address the following three critical concerns:

- **Pricing**: Prices must be realistic and supported. The report should reflect consideration of both price inflation and cost inflation over the estimated life of the properties.

- **Discount factors**: Discount rates should reflect current market interest rates.

- **Timing**: Reports should be accurate and should represent the production of the mineral interest. In most instances, the report should not exceed 12 months. Significant price fluctuations or changes in interest rates may require adjustments to the valuation of the reserves to reflect current conditions. The critical factor in determining the adequacy of the timeliness of the report is change in market conditions.

A broad range of market factors may affect the value of mineral interests, including supply and demand for refined products and leasing activity both in the immediate area and globally. The type of valuation needed depends on how the asset is to be used. Formal valuations are typically performed by geologists or petroleum engineers and are very costly. Bank fiduciaries generally obtain engineering reports for estate tax purposes, or when large interests are purchased, sold, or used for collateral for borrowing. Bank fiduciaries may use an informal value of three-to-five years' historical production, along with an analysis of market factors. These less formal valuations may be used for risk assessments for small fractional interests or properties that the bank trust department management is familiar with, and before the sale of older, smaller interests. The bank's policy should set guidelines for when a certain valuation process may be used.

Mineral interests, such as depleting assets, are difficult to value because the price is based on the assets' continued availability at any given time. It has been industry practice to list each mineral property on the trust department's master asset listing at a nominal $1 value. While this valuation method may be simpler, it is not likely to reflect the significance of the assets being managed. Bank fiduciaries therefore should use caution when following this practice and need to ensure they have other valuation methods in place.

Technological advances may lead to an increase in production in wells that were once not economically viable. Because of this, it is industry practice to retain mineral interests, if the instrument authorizes retaining them without liability to the fiduciary.

Fiduciaries usually charge a set fee for minerals management rather than a percentage of market value. Minerals management fees should be based on the risks associated with the specific type of holding and the resources required to manage it. Banks should refer to OCC Asset Management Interpretation on Call Report Schedule RC-T – Mineral Properties (January 14, 2005), for more details regarding the use of multiples of annual revenues in the context valuations for Call Report filings. The document can be found at www.occ.gov/topics/capital-markets/asset-management/corporate-trust/memo-rc-t-mineral-properties.pdf.

Leases

The bank fiduciary is responsible for negotiating mineral leases. A lease is a legal document in which the holder of the mineral interests on a specified tract of land grants either specific individuals or companies the right to enter the property and to conduct a search for oil and gas. Leases address the terms of the arrangement and how revenue and the liability are portioned. Some terms may change depending on market factors. When negotiating a new lease, the fiduciary should try to obtain information about the terms of other recent leases on comparable mineral interests in the area from other operators.

When negotiating a new lease, the bank fiduciary should use a lease document prepared by legal counsel. If the bank fiduciary is using a standard lease drafted by the operator (lessee), at a minimum, bank legal counsel or counsel with expertise should review all lease documents before execution. Standardized lease forms provided by the lessee may not contain language needed to fully protect the interests of the fiduciary account and the bank fiduciary. Some common features found in leases include

- a provision for a fixed-term, often three years.

- an up-front cash bonus (paid on a per-acre basis) to the lessor (trust account) on signing.

- a provision within the terms of the lease that provides the lessee the option to either drill or pay "delay rentals." "Delay rentals" are payments by the operator to the lessor to extend the terms of the lease in the absence of production. (These payments are generally contractually required to hold the lease.)

- royalty provisions in the event the well starts producing.

- the total depth to which the lessee is allowed to drill without an increase in the percentage royalty payment.

- conflicts of interest language stating that the lessees are not related to the bank, its shareholders, directors, officers, or other interested parties.

While state laws vary, in oil-rich states like Texas and Oklahoma, an oil company with a minerals lease has the right to explore for minerals and is not required to obtain permission from the surface owner. The oil or gas company usually attempts, however, to obtain the surface owner's agreement to avoid legal issues later. Bank fiduciaries that own the surface where exploration is occurring should negotiate a "surface damage agreement" with the operator. The agreement not only sets out how the surface owner is compensated in case of property damage but also establishes parameters for ingress and egress to the land.

Managing Income and Expenses

The amount of income received from a producing property depends on several factors; including the fraction of the interest owned, lease terms, and the level of production. If the oil or gas well is established, with regular production expected from the well, the bank fiduciary may receive monthly royalty checks. Otherwise, companies sometimes aggregate small payments until they reach a reasonable amount, usually agreed upon in advance, or they may issue one annual check.

For working interests, the bank fiduciary may receive authorization for expenditures (AFE) from the operator (expenses for developing the interest), which the bank fiduciary must approve and return to the operator. Before approving an AFE, the bank fiduciary should be knowledgeable about the industry, the operations of the particular interest, and the operator to ensure that the expenses being approved are reasonable. The bank should have a system in place for allocating payments between principal and income.

Federal and state tax laws establish depletion allowances for tax purposes and an array of other taxation issues. Accounting for mineral depletion and allocation of payments between principal and income beneficiaries are usually established by state law.

The bank fiduciary should have a process for managing income and expenses associated with the extraction of mineral interests. The bank should obtain the information needed and have appropriate systems or processes in place to anticipate the timing and estimated amount of income payments. If a payment is not received or the amount is unusual, this should prompt further inquiry from the department. The bank fiduciary should also have good internal controls over income posting and check writing as with any other income producing property.

Environmental Issues

Working interests have the greatest potential liability. The bank fiduciary should ensure that any working interest lease requires that the operator maintain environmental liability insurance. If possible, the bank fiduciary should require annual documentation showing the bank fiduciary as an "additional insured." Maintaining environmental liability insurance mitigates the need to perform environmental assessments of the drilling or mining sites. Inspections of these types of properties are extremely important and may warrant inspections more frequently than annually.

Closely Held Businesses

A closely held business is one that is owned by a single or small number of persons. Closely held businesses may be organized in various legal forms, such as closely held corporations, partnerships, sole proprietorships, or limited liability companies. Below are some examples of closely held business structures.

Closely Held Corporation

A closely held corporation is a corporation whose stock is owned by a limited number of shareholders and is not actively traded on any local market or major exchange. A closely held corporation is contrasted with a publicly held corporation, which often has thousands or even millions of shareholders who are able to buy and sell their shares in public markets. A publicly held corporation is a registered entity with the U.S. Securities and Exchange Commission (SEC). As a registered entity, a publicly held corporation is subject to the SEC's periodic financial reporting requirements. Closely held corporations are not registered with the SEC and are not subject to the SEC's periodic financial reporting requirements.

The organization and laws governing the internal affairs of closely held corporations are the same as for publicly held corporations. A corporation is created by filing a certificate of formation with the Secretary of State in the state where the corporation is physically located or where the company legally elects to incorporate. A corporation is regarded as a legal person and has the attributes of limited liability, centralization of management, perpetual duration, and ease of transferability of shares. The owners of a corporation are called "shareholders." The persons who manage the business and affairs of a corporation are called "directors."

Partnerships

- **General partnership**: An association of two or more persons, all of whom are general partners. Each partner is jointly and separately liable for the partnership's obligations. Each partner takes a share in the profits or losses of the partnership. Partners have equal control of the business. A general partnership may arise informally, although the sound practice is to define the relationships among the general partners in a written partnership agreement. Because of the unlimited liability of general partners, a bank trustee would normally not accept a general partnership as a trust asset.

- **Limited partnership**: A partnership with two types of partners, general partners and limited partners. A limited partnership is created in accordance with the requirements of state law, including the filing of a limited partnership certificate with the state. The general partners have the same rights as noted in the previous paragraph, and they are responsible for the operation of the limited partnership. The limited partners have limited liability based on their investment in the business. The general partners in a limited partnership recognize profits and losses jointly and severally, as they do in a general partnership. Limited partners only recognize profits and losses in proportion to their investment. The remainder goes to the general partners. As noted in the previous paragraph, a bank typically serves only as a limited partner for liability reasons.

- **Family-limited partnership** (FLP): A form of limited partnership generally created to manage and control family properties or businesses. These partnerships are usually established as part of an inter-generational wealth transfer strategy. Two primary benefits for establishing an FLP are

  - to "fractionalize" interests in property (turning property into units of a partnership) for the purpose of carrying out a gifting strategy.
  - to seek "discounts" on gifts made as well as on the transfer of a partner's remaining interest in the FLP at death. These benefits of an FLP may reduce estate taxes.

An FLP allows persons to transfer personal or business assets into a partnership and then grant limited ownership interests to their children or other family members. Although assets are merely transferred from one account to another, this type of partnership was established historically to reduce the estate's taxable value. The transfer to the FLP of, for example, publicly traded securities, lowers the value of the overall portfolio by making the underlying properties less liquid. In addition, a grantor can ensure that these assets remain in the family as long as they remain owned by the partnership. There is generally a limited market for these assets because of their concentrated ownership, typically within one family. Many of these partnerships, however, are formed to hold assets for tax reasons, not to sell them. In light of recent rulings that limit the tax advantages of FLPs, partnerships should have valid non-tax reasons to exist, such as managing a family business or pooling together investment assets (real estate, for example). In addition, the creators of the FLPs should not use partnership assets, such as cash or a house, for personal use. If a grantor donates to a partnership but still continues to use assets, the assets *may* revert back to the grantor's estate.

- **Joint venture**: A business structure formed by two or more parties for a specific purpose. Joint ventures are similar to partnerships but are usually limited to one or two projects.

- **Sole proprietorship**: Although not a partnership, it is legal form of business that makes no legal distinction between the individual owner and the business itself. The owner takes all the profits and losses and is personally liable for the business obligations. Income and losses from sole proprietorships are reported on the owner's personal federal tax return. In contrast, income or losses from other forms of corporate ownership are reported on separate returns with each entity's own taxpayer identification number.

- **Limited liability company** (LLC): A hybrid legal form of business (corporation and limited partnership combined) that is taxed by the IRS as a sole proprietorship with the same limited liability attribute of a corporation. LLC owners are called "members." The management structure must be stated in the certificate of formation filed with the state where it is based, similar to a corporation, but the LLC operates under an operating agreement similar to a partnership agreement.

A bank fiduciary's administration of closely held businesses in the various legal forms can be complex. The level of its responsibilities and its ability to exercise control varies with the percent of ownership. A trust department that manages these types of assets must have well-developed policies and procedures to ensure sound and prudent administration as well as safeguards against potential liability. This may require more bank management oversight. The bank fiduciary may be held liable by account beneficiaries for any losses incurred from mismanaging these assets. Mismanagement can occur if the bank does not have the expertise to operate a certain type of business and does not seek outside managers to provide the expertise. The fact that closely held businesses generally have limited marketability, or a sale may require approval of other owners, gives the bank limited options for addressing difficult situations. Often times, a grantor, surviving spouse, or beneficiary is involved in running the business or is employed by the business.

A bank fiduciary should document the type of business and provide a comprehensive analysis of each business's financial condition, management, earnings, growth, marketability, product lines or services, and competitors. Additionally, the bank should periodically request financial information from the business, develop a method for evaluating the business's financial condition annually, and document reasons for continuing to hold or sell the asset. Closely held businesses, when held as investments, should be suitable for the account and in line with the account's investment objectives.

The governing trust instrument often contains specific language regarding the disposition of a closely held business that is received in kind or deposited. If the instrument is silent, the bank fiduciary must act in the best interests of the beneficiaries and determine whether to continue to operate the business. Bank fiduciaries that have sole investment discretion over an account that is the majority owner of a closely held company are in a position to control the company. If, however, the trust account holds only a minority interest or shares responsibilities with other co-fiduciaries, a bank fiduciary can be placed in a position of negotiating with co-fiduciaries over the best course for the business going forward.

In some situations, it may be in the best interest of the account beneficiaries for a bank fiduciary officer to be a member of the company's board of directors so the bank fiduciary can influence decisions affecting the company. Fees received by the bank fiduciary for serving as a board member should be remitted to the account unless otherwise negotiated. The bank may only retain the fee if specifically authorized by applicable law. In addition, the bank should ensure it is acting at arm's length to avoid any self-dealing transactions or even the appearance of a conflict of interest. Such conflicts could arise if the bank is lending the company money or if bank personnel acquire an interest, financial or otherwise, in the company. A bank fiduciary may potentially assume additional liability by serving as a director or officer for a company if the decisions they are involved in cause harm to the company. Bank fiduciaries should obtain directors liability insurance when acting in this capacity.

Evidence of Ownership

Management should maintain documentation that establishes the bank's legal capacity as bank fiduciary of any closely held business assets. This documentation must reflect the form of the company's incorporation, such as a stock certificate registered with the Secretary of State in the state where the corporation is located. Partnership interests also need to be registered to reflect the bank's ownership interest held in its fiduciary capacity.

Valuations

The bank should have a sound process to determine when a formal valuation is obtained. The need to determine the value of ownership interests in closely held business assets arises in a number of situations. For example, the following all require that a value be placed on the business as an ongoing concern: the sale of the stock of a closely owned company; the sale of interests in a partnership business; diversification into more liquid assets; tax calculations; marital and corporate dissolutions; buy-sell agreements; stock option plans; recapitalizations; and succession planning. The bank fiduciary must be able to demonstrate that a reasonable approach was taken in valuing these assets. IRS Revenue Ruling 59–60 provides general guidance on valuing stocks of closely held assets where market quotations are not available.

The bank fiduciary must also have current fair market values of these assets for its quarterly reporting on Schedule RC-T in the bank's call report, as well as for assets held in an IRA. Formal appraisals are needed when an ownership interest is claimed as a charitable donation or as part of an employee stock ownership plan. In addition, an accurate valuation is required under 12 CFR 9.6(c) and 12 CFR 150.220 to conduct an annual investment review on a fiduciary account for which the bank has discretion.

Insurance

Insurance coverage required for closely held business assets depends on the type of business. The bank fiduciary is responsible for determining what type and amount of coverage is needed based on the nature of the business and its fair market value. For example, a closely held corporation that manufactures goods requires different insurance coverage than an accounting firm set up as a limited partnership. In the former example, the bank fiduciary should be named as "loss payee" on the policy for the manufacturing firm, whereas the accounting firm may need a higher level of "professional liability insurance." A review of these policies should be done during the annual investment review of the account to ensure there is adequate coverage based on asset type. If the bank fiduciary has an employee representative serving on the board of a closely held company, the bank should obtain insurance for that person, as well as the bank in its capacity as fiduciary, to protect against potential liability that could result from actions taken by the board.

Administering these types of investments requires an effective risk management process. This process should include

- standards addressing the retention and, on a rare occasion, a possible purchase of a minority ownership interest in a closely held business and a means to communicate those standards to appropriate bank personnel.

- documentation to support retention of closely held companies, including letters of direction, when appropriate, and confirmation that any proposed purchase of closely held stock is permitted by the governing instrument.

- an approval process that involves the trust committee or senior management for any purchase and retention decisions regarding investments in ownership interests in a closely held business.

- a pre-acceptance legal review of documents to assess the risk exposure to the bank and to identify any real or potential conflicts of interest.

- Identification of potential BSA/AML issues that need to be addressed, depending on the type of business the entity is engaged in.

Loans and Notes

Loans and notes held as assets in fiduciary accounts include mortgages, real estate notes secured by deeds of trust, other secured notes, unsecured loans, and employee benefit participant loans. Loans and notes in personal trust accounts can be brought in with the account as part of the assets received at inception, or they can be acquired later at the request of the grantor. The bank fiduciary may make loans if allowed by the governing instrument. A bank is prohibited from making a loan from a trust account to an officer, director, or employee of the bank 12 USC 92a(h) (for national banks) and 12 USC 1464(n)(7) (for federal savings associations).

The bank fiduciary is responsible for collecting payment, securing and inspecting collateral, and, if the note is secured by real property, ensuring the timely payment of taxes and verifying that insurance coverage is current and adequate. In addition, in the event of nonpayment, the bank is responsible for foreclosure or debt collection processes.

Real estate loans may be appropriate fiduciary investments as long as the bank fiduciary carefully considers both the short- and long-term liquidity needs of the account. A factor to consider for a bank fiduciary is whether the real estate securing the loan provides adequate security to cover the principal and interest of the loan and whether there is an analysis of the borrower's capacity to repay the loan. While loans and notes generally have a higher yield than short-term debt securities, loans and notes generally also have longer maturities and less liquidity than other more traditional investments in a trust account, such as stocks or bonds. They are not readily marketable and may require large capital outlays compared to other investments and inspection of the collateral also required.

A bank may not make real estate loans that the bank subsequently sells to discretionary trust accounts, unless the loans are earmarked at inception for this purpose and acquisition is specifically authorized in the trust instrument and applicable law. Where authorized, a bank fiduciary may invest fiduciary assets in real estate loans in situations where the bank has provided the construction financing for a project and the bank has made a firm commitment at the time of the construction loan to take over the permanent financing. It is important to note, however, that this is a prohibited transaction under ERISA for employee benefit trusts, as this would be considered a transaction between the account and a party in interest in contravention of ERISA Section 406(a). See the "Retirement Plan Services" booklet of the *Comptroller's Handbook* for an in-depth discussion of prohibited transactions under ERISA and potential liability affecting parties in interest.

When making decisions concerning real estate loans or other collateralized loans, a fiduciary should ensure that

- real estate values are supported by current appraisals and inspections.

- the loan to current appraised value of the real property is an acceptable ratio.

- Uniform Commercial Code filings for collateral have been made with appropriate state offices, in most cases, the state's Secretary of State's office, and ticklers are in place to identify expiration of those filings.

- the borrower's ability to pay has been established.

- documentation necessary to establish priority of lien and validity of loan is in place.

- adequate insurance on the underlying property is obtained and a proper loss-payee clause is included.

- ticklers for proper controls are established that address dates for loan payments, taxes, insurance premium payments, Uniform Commercial Code filings, inspections.

- adequate interest rates are charged.

Life Insurance

Life insurance may be placed in a trust as part of an estate planning tool. Life insurance policies may be put into a trust to remove the policy from a grantor's estate for inheritance or estate transfer tax purposes. A life insurance policy frequently provides the surviving beneficiaries with a liquid asset to pay estate taxes and other final expenses, while enabling them to retain other less liquid assets in the estate. Bank fiduciaries are responsible for protecting and managing the life insurance policy for the benefit of the beneficiaries for the life of the grantor. A bank fiduciary must understand each life insurance policy that the trust accepts or purchases, or the bank fiduciary must employ an advisor who is qualified, independent, objective, and not affiliated with an insurance company to prudently manage these assets. In addition, the bank fiduciary must periodically review the financial condition and rating of the insurance company. The majority of these policies are deposited into the trust by the grantor. Many states have recently passed legislation to limit the liability of bank fiduciaries, in certain situations, by rescinding requirements under state law to perform due diligence on insurance companies as a directed bank fiduciary. The OCC, however, continues to require bank fiduciaries to follow 12 CFR 9.6(c) and 12 CFR 150.220 and to conduct annual investment reviews of all assets of each fiduciary account for which the bank has investment discretion. This review should evaluate the financial health of the issuing insurance company as well as whether the policy is performing as illustrated or whether replacement should be considered.

Life insurance trusts are frequently used as estate planning tools. These trusts involve ownership of a life insurance policy that is transferred to a trust by the grantor, and the trust is then identified as the designated beneficiary of the policy. If certain conditions are met, the policy proceeds may pass outside of the grantor's estate thus escaping estate transfer taxes. There are numerous scenarios, however, where IRS rules could result in a clawback of these policies to the grantor's estate preventing individuals, for example, from gifting assets to their descendants or other parties once death is imminent in an attempt to avoid estate taxes. These rules primarily focus on insurance policies or assets in which the deceased retains an interest. Absent an irrevocable life insurance trust (ILIT) or some other tax avoidance arrangement, the proceeds of the life insurance policy would otherwise be taxable.

Using an ILIT can result in a significant portion of an estate passing untaxed to the beneficiaries by avoiding federal estate taxes on the proceeds. In addition to transferring an existing policy to this type of trust, it is possible to create the trust and then have the trust apply for a life insurance policy. In this situation, the current federal tax code provides that there is no three-year waiting period before the tax advantages are achieved.

The possible tax savings of an ILIT are its major advantage. There are, however, some specific requirements that must be considered before a bank trust department accepts and manages such assets:

- The trust must be irrevocable. Once the policy is transferred to the trust, the trust cannot be amended or revoked by the person setting up the trust (the insured).

- Allowing the policy to lapse can present a substantial problem. The fiduciary may be unable to obtain replacement insurance because the insured party has become uninsurable, or may only be able to obtain insurance coverage at a significantly higher cost because the insured party has moved into a different risk category.

- An ILIT typically includes provisions (called "Crummey Provisions" after an IRS case) that allow a beneficiary to withdraw any contribution made to the trust, e.g. contributions to cover premium payments. These special withdrawal powers must be very carefully drafted to avoid creating tax problems for the trust. See the "Personal Fiduciary Services" booklet of the *Comptroller's Handbook* for details on these types of trusts (appendix A, pages 72-73).

Adequacy of Insurance Assets

Bank fiduciaries need to have well-developed risk management practices to evaluate and administer accounts with insurance policy holdings. A bank fiduciary with discretion over the account must complete formal pre-acceptance, initial post-acceptance and annual reviews of the insurance policy. Independent of these reviews, a fiduciary bank must have risk management systems and reviews that address the following.

- **Sufficiency of premiums**: The bank fiduciary must determine whether current premiums are sufficient to maintain the policy to maturity or to meet the insured's life expectancy.

- **Suitability of the insurance policy**: Consider replacing an insurance policy if the bank fiduciary identifies concerns with the condition of the insurance provider or if that provider does not meet the needs of the grantor or beneficiaries. Also assess any tax changes that could affect the suitability of the policy.

- **Carrier selection**: The bank fiduciary needs to evaluate the carrier's financial condition. To the extent insurance carrier ratings are available, they generally lag corporate and market events, and should be used principally as indicators of a firm's creditworthiness.

- **Appropriateness of investment strategy**: The bank fiduciary must evaluate the appropriateness of investments of any segregated account to support the cash value.

For policies with flexible premiums and nonguaranteed benefits, the trustee should obtain the original policy illustration, which shows planned premium strategies. This policy illustration is subject to a high degree of fluctuation. Periodically, the trustee should obtain an in-force illustration. This provides a measure of performance of a life insurance policy against what was initially illustrated. By obtaining an in-force illustration, the trustee can monitor the effectiveness of the policy to date and project how the policy may perform in the future and plan for any potential shortfall in premiums. This process assists the trustee in monitoring the economics of the policy.

Generally, while insurance companies are regulated by the state and maintain a mandatory level of reserves, specific assets are not identified to support an insurer's promise to pay on a policy. Policyholders are subject to the creditworthiness and liquidity constraints of the company. It is important that a bank fiduciary perform due diligence on an insurance company issuing a policy to ensure that it is sound, viable and able to meet future obligations.

Cash value on permanent life insurance policies may be included as part of the account's assets if the bank has done a thorough review of the insurance company's financial condition and is satisfied with its soundness. The cash values for variable life and variable universal life policies, however, are supported by separate accounts and comprise assets selected by the policyholder and should be included as account assets. Other term type policies should be held at a nominal value because the payment and value of those policies is based on the payment ability of the insurance company at a future date. Insurance policies should never be reported at the face value of the policy. In some instances, the bank may just hold a policy for safekeeping, see further discussion of different types of insurance products in appendix E of this booklet.

Tangible Assets and Collectibles

Tangible assets include household furnishings and automobiles. Collectibles include works of art, antiques, stamps, coins and bullion, gemstones, and other miscellaneous assets. These assets are generally found in estates and personal trusts. There are restrictions on collectibles in IRAs and employee benefit accounts. The governing instrument should authorize retention and possible purchase of tangible assets. Appraisals should be obtained upon receipt of such assets and valuations must be updated periodically. Depending on the terms of the governing instrument and the specific needs of the trust, tangible assets and collectibles are usually either distributed in kind to designated beneficiaries or are sold to provide liquidity. Bank fiduciaries must provide strong internal controls, appropriate storage, adequate insurance, and accurate values for these physical assets.

Collectibles such as rare stamps and coins should be authenticated by experts. Diamonds and other gemstones require certificates of authenticity from gemologists or other expert appraisers. It is essential that such assets be maintained under dual control and be protected from theft, substitution, and physical damage. Because of their unique nature, these assets may be irreplaceable. The bank should be aware of specific requirements for storage of certain types of assets, such as furs, firearms, or liquor. For some types of tangible assets and collectibles, appropriate off-site storage should be considered. With some notable exceptions, tangible assets may be difficult to liquidate. Before accepting unusually rare or highly valuable collectibles, bank fiduciaries should consider whether it is appropriate to verify the authenticity and provenance of the asset and whether there are applicable laws or regulations that restrict the disposition of the asset. Federal and state laws, the Federal Bureau of Investigation's Art Crime Team, and numerous other domestic and foreign law enforcement groups have been established to assist in locating, identifying, and securing the return of art, artifacts, and cultural properties to their rightful owners.

The following procedures are intended to assist examiners in determining the quantity of risk and the quality of risk management when examining unique assets in an asset management department. The procedures supplement and amplify core assessment procedures found in the "Community Bank Supervision" and "Large Bank Supervision" booklets of the *Comptroller's Handbook*. Examiners should determine which of these procedures to perform during the examination planning process, depending on the complexity and risks associated with the unique assets held in a bank's asset management department. The decision to use expanded procedures is coordinated with the asset management examiner responsible for planning fiduciary examination activities for the applicable bank and must be adequately documented in the work papers.

Planning Activities

Objective: To review the quantity of risk and quality of risk management relating to the management of unique assets and to establish the timing, scope, and work plans for this supervisory activity.

1. Consult the following sources of information, if applicable, and review the types and risk characteristics of the unique assets managed by the bank:

   • OCC information systems.

   • Previous reports of examination, related management responses, and work papers.

   • Asset management profile.

   • Complaints and litigation concerning management of unique assets.

   • Audit, compliance reports, other risk monitoring reports, and management responses provided to the board, committees, business line managers, and risk management groups.

2. Request and analyze trust department unique asset reports to identify

trends, growth, and oversight of this area since the last examination. See appendix A for a sample Request Letter.

3. Develop a preliminary risk assessment and discuss it with the functional Examiner-in-Charge (FEIC) for asset management or the bank Examiner-in-Charge (EIC) for perspective and examination planning and coordination.

4. Depending on the performance of the previous steps, combined with discussions with the FEIC and other appropriate supervisors, determine the examination scope and the necessary amount of testing.

5. Select from the following examination procedures the necessary steps to meet examination objectives and supervisory strategy.

Quantity of Risk

Conclusion: The quantity of risk is (low, moderate, or high).

Objective: To determine the quantity of risk associated with the management of unique assets.

1. Obtain and analyze management information reports relating to transaction processing and reporting in the management of unique assets. Consider the following structural factors:

   - The volume, type, and complexity of transactions, products, and services offered with respect to unique assets.

   - The various systems and reports used for control and oversight of unique assets.

2. Obtain and review the most recently completed audit and compliance reports covering unique asset activities and the last OCC examination report:

   - Discuss the findings and recommendations relating to the management of unique assets with OCC examiners and bank management.

   - Determine whether management has taken corrective action to address previous concerns and to implement OCC recommendations.

3. Select for review a sample of each substantial unique asset category over which the bank exercises investment discretion. The sample should include both recently accepted unique assets as well as existing unique assets. Complete a review of each unique asset and review the following factors relevant to each category:

   New Assets Factors

   - Compliance with the bank's due diligence acceptance process and policy.

   - Compliance with applicable federal, state and local laws.

- Appropriate holdings for the account and consideration whether they are in accordance with the trust legal document.

- Appropriateness of title for real property, mineral interests, and appropriate state registration for closely held assets.

- Environmental assessment, if needed or warranted.

- Adequate ticklers to establish documentation necessary to effectively control and manage the unique assets type.

Existing Assets Factors

- Valuations are updated periodically, according to a consistent risk-based process.

- Annual account reviews are performed to ensure each unique asset is appropriate for the account as a whole.

- Inspections of properties are performed annually.

- Real estate tax payments are current.

- Insurance payments are current and coverage is adequate.

- Assets are made productive, unless trust instrument states otherwise.

- Financial analysis is performed annually of income-producing properties, closely held businesses, and working mineral interests.

- Review of industry associated with unique assets is performed to compare financial performance.

- Expenditures for capital improvements are appropriate and receive necessary approvals.

- For insurance trusts an analysis of insurer solvency/strength and adequacy of policy(s) reflects any changes in grantor circumstances.

4. Select a sample of unique assets that has been purchased or sold since the last examination. Review the following:

- Independent appraisal or valuation of asset.

- Appropriateness of sale based on the account's investment objectives and trust agreement.

- Conflicts of interest with either outside parties or agents to the transaction or bank insiders.

- Sale transaction at arm's length, fair, with proper disclosures of fees and costs.

- Appropriate board or appointed committee that reviewed and approved sale or purchase.

Quality of Risk Management

Conclusion: The quality of risk management is (strong, satisfactory, or weak).

Policies

Objective: Determine whether the board has established adequate policies, which are appropriate for the complexity and scope of the bank's management of unique assets.

1. Review policy guidelines developed by the bank to ensure the proper administration of unique assets. Guidelines should address

   - types of unique assets the bank is willing to accept or purchase for fiduciary accounts.

   - acceptance/pre-approval process.

   - assessment of environmental liability for real estate, closely held companies, and mineral interests.

   - how unique assets are incorporated into the annual account investment review (OCC Bulletin 2008-10, "Fiduciary Activities of National Banks: Annual Reviews of Fiduciary Accounts Pursuant to 12 CFR 9.6(c)"and 12 CFR 150.220).

   - compliance with applicable federal, state and local laws.

   - valuation/appraisal standards and time frames.

   - periodic inspections.

   - maintenance and capital improvements of real estate and closely held businesses and working interests.

   - process for administering life insurance policies held by a trust, how the department ensures that the policy is appropriate, and systems are in place to ensure no lapse in coverage occurs.

- process for monitoring the condition of the insurance company and plan of action, if deterioration is detected.

2. Assess how the board of directors or trust committee periodically reviews, updates, and approves unique assets policies. Assess how the board ensures that policies are consistent with the bank's strategic direction and risk tolerance.

Processes

Objective: Assess the quality of unique assets supervision practices, procedures, and internal controls.

1. Evaluate how unique assets policies, procedures, and plans are communicated to personnel. Examples of effective methods used by trust departments include

- communicating policies and expectations to appropriate personnel in a timely and concise manner.

- periodic internal training sessions to review current policy guidelines and update personnel about regulatory and corresponding policy changes.

- approval and monitoring of compliance with policies and management responsiveness to regulatory, industry, and technology changes.

2. Determine which processes are in place (such as checklists, tickler systems, review forms, and exception reporting) to ensure

- timely performance of valuations and inspections.

- environmental inspections.

- maintenance of adequate insurance.

- payment of real estate taxes.

- proper safeguarding of tangible assets and collectibles.

- appropriate information about unique assets is provided to personnel performing the annual account investment review and other types of reviews.

- timely follow-up of reporting and tracking of exceptions.

3. Assess the quality of inspections, valuations, and review information. Pay particular attention to areas requiring special expertise, such as farm and ranch management, timber management, commercial real estate, life insurance, and closely held businesses.

4. For farm and ranch properties, determine whether controls implemented to safeguard and verify farm commodities are adequate.

5. Determine whether processes are in place to ensure compliance with policy. Examples of effective processes include committee oversight, peer reviews, and officer approval requirements.

Personnel

Objective: Determine whether personnel demonstrate the expertise and skills needed to effectively manage unique assets, with a focus on assets requiring specialized expertise (such as mineral interest, farm property or significant interests in closely held businesses).

1. Evaluate the adequacy of personnel resources, given the volume and complexity of the different unique assets. Assess the impact of turnover of personnel overseeing these unique assets areas.

2. Assess the bank's policy on providing continuing education to ensure that personnel stay current on regulatory changes and industry standards.

3. Determine whether the bank employs agents (for example, realtors, environmental specialists, or property managers) to manage or perform an administrative function, asset valuation, or inspection for the department's unique assets services.

   The bank's process for selecting outside agents/vendors, if they provide a significant service to the department, should include factors identified in the OCC Bulletin 2001-47, "Third-Party Relationships: Risk Management Principles":

- Agent/vendor due diligence review.

- Contract negotiations and approvals.

- Vendor monitoring, including the frequency and quality of information reviewed.

- Identification of personnel to serve as points of contact with the agent/vendor and to conduct ongoing monitoring.

4. Determine whether the bank's evaluation and compensation programs consider individuals' and trust department's compliance with policy guidelines.

Control Systems

Objectives: Determine whether effective control systems are in place to monitor compliance with established unique assets management policies and processes. Determine whether control systems identify, measure, and monitor risk.

1. Assess the adequacy of management information systems. Consider the following factors when assessing the quality of reports:

- Appropriateness of type of information provided.

- Accuracy of data.

- Timeliness of reporting.

- Adequate level of detail.

- Organization and depth of analysis.

2. Determine the effectiveness of audit or compliance reviews of unique assets management. A good quality audit has the following:

- A risk-based scope and frequency of reviews based on the types of unique assets the bank administers and the number of these types of assets in the department.

- Reported weaknesses prioritized on the basis of risk to the bank.

- Recommendations for corrective action. Responsibility for corrective action assigned to a person and given a time frame within which to accomplish corrective action.

- Follow-up method to measure the effectiveness of corrective action.

3. Determine whether the compliance function provides the following:

- Risk assessment of the unique assets area.

- Information for personnel about changes in regulations and industry standards.

- Measures of unique assets management's compliance with bank policy, regulations, and prudent fiduciary practices.

Conclusion

Complete the examination of unique assets management.

Objective: Determine overall conclusions and communicate findings regarding the quantity of risk and management's ability to identify, measure, monitor, and control risk in unique assets management.

1. Prepare a summary memorandum to the asset management examiner or EIC regarding the types, quantity, direction of risk, and the adequacy of risk management for the unique assets area.

2. Recommend risk assessments for the unique assets portfolio. Refer to the "Community Bank Supervision" and "Large Bank Supervision" booklets of the *Comptroller's Handbook*.

3. Discuss examination findings and conclusions with the EIC.

4. Discuss findings with bank management, including conclusions about risks. If necessary, obtain commitments for corrective action.

5. Based on discussions with the EIC, bank management, and information contained in the summary memorandum; prepare a unique assets management comment for inclusion in the report of examination "ROE." If necessary, compose "Matters Requiring Attention" (MRA) for the ROE.

6. Provide any necessary information to the asset management examiner to update the supervisory record.

7. Prepare an updated supervisory strategy for unique assets and provide it to the asset management FEIC for review, approval, and submission to the EIC.

8. Prepare a memorandum or update work programs with any information that facilitates future examinations.

9. Organize and reference work papers in accordance with OCC guidelines.

Appendix A: Request Letter (Sample)

Please provide request items in digital electronic format if possible.

1. Copy of the most recent organizational chart for unique assets. Include geographic distribution of associates and departments and the names of compliance or risk management associates assigned to this function.

2. Outline of committee structure for committees that oversee unique assets (valuation committee, approval committee, specific product line committees, etc.) and any associated work groups. Include meeting frequency, members, and minutes for the previous and most current year.

3. Current policies and procedures for accepting and managing and valuing unique assets such as real estate, mineral interests, farm and ranch, timberland, closely held businesses, insurance, and collectibles.

4. List of accounts containing unique assets broken out by the categories noted in item 3. Describe how managers are assigned to the different asset lines (geographically? company type? dollar size? industry?).

5. Unique assets reports denoting asset volume, market value, and revenue for the primary unique assets categories.

6. Policies and procedures for inspections and valuations of properties. Describe the types of appraisals and whether performed externally or internally (include forms used if performed in-house). Describe approval processes when determining the type of appraisals to be used and who approves.

7. Policies and procedures for determining valuations of closely held business assets. Include valuation forms used if performed in-house. Also describe the approval processes for accepting or rejecting asset valuations.

8. Copy of the most recent internal unique assets audit and associated management response. Include the most recent compliance testing and reporting performed in the unique assets areas.

9. A listing or discussion of all outstanding and pending litigation and formal complaints related to unique or specialty assets.

10. Reports on any charge-offs or write-downs related to the administration of unique assets.

11. List and briefly describe the primary systems used to support various types of unique assets (for example, accounting systems for oil and gas properties). Detail any vendor management arrangements the bank has for these products, specifically targeting those that deal with managing or providing support for the different asset types.

12. Briefly describe any new products, services, or activities being planned in this area. Include any current marketing materials.

13. Provide access to training program and materials used in any training for this product line.

14. Describe how ILITs are administered. Provide policies and procedures and management supervision of this product line. Also include a listing of accounts holding insurance.

15. If the bank relies on legal opinions interpreting state laws when offering ILITs, please provide opinions.

Appendix B: Environmental Inspections

There are three phases of environmental inspections. Phase one is a visual inspection. Phase two involves testing for contamination. Phase three is actual cleanup.

Phase One

An environmental professional prepares phase-one audits. A professional has special experience and training. The phase-one audit is designed to identify the presence of substances such as radon, asbestos, leaking underground storage tanks, polychlorinated biphenyls (PCB), lead-based paint, and contaminated groundwater. Typical property sites that may evidence these types of contamination are gas stations, convenience stores, landfills, print shops, laundries and dry cleaners, auto repair and body shops, and farms. The scope of a phase-one audit includes

- a review of property ownership and use during the past 60 years to determine whether the presence of any hazardous waste exists or is possible.

- use of aerial images to look at land contours that may help determine use of the property and adjacent property.

- a closer visual inspection of the property, including all structures, facilities, improvements, and adjacent land.

- a review of federal, state, and local government records for any mention of hazardous waste.

- a recommendation for a phase-two audit, if the phase-one review indicated the likelihood or threatened release of hazardous waste.

Phase Two

A phase-two audit includes various segments of a phase-one audit, but extends to actual testing of soil and water for contamination. Other tests performed include, as appropriate, an analysis of acid mine drainage, testing of underground storage tanks, and testing for asbestos materials.

Phase Three

A phase-three audit requires additional testing of the site with the objective of estimating the cost of cleaning up the site. During this phase, state environmental authorities must be notified that a contaminated site has been identified.

Appendix C

Real Estate Worksheet					
This worksheet can help examiners who are following the real estate procedures.					
Account name:			Account type:		
Account number:			Administrator:		
Address of property:					
Date of last inspection:		Condition of property:			
Date and value of last appraisal:					
System carrying value:		Fee calculation based on:			
Income-producing:		Non-income-producing:		Vacant land:	
Environmental issues					
1.	Items to consider when acquiring or retaining a property (check if considered and no issues found; highlight any deficiencies):				
		• Property occupied/managed by grantor or beneficiary.			
		• Condition of title.			
		• Current appraisal by a qualified appraiser.			
		• Inspection reports.			
		• Current yield, income, and expense records.			
		• Leases and rents, including status of delinquent rents.			
		• Cost of maintenance, repairs, and capital improvements.			
		• Annual inspection/condition of property.			
		• Proper insurance.			
		• Taxes current.			
		• Potential liability for environmental risks.			

2.	Does the bank determine the condition of the title to real property under administration in accounts with investment responsibility? (Use N/A—not applicable—if exempt.)	
3.	Are the following items considered when the bank makes a recommendation or attempt to sell real estate?	
		Current appraisals by competent appraisers.
		Comparable sales analysis.
		Use of multiple listings, when appropriate.
4.	If a management agent is employed, determine whether the management agency agreement	
		adequately establishes the agent's duties and responsibilities, frequency of reporting, and commission charges.
		has been approved by bank legal counsel.
5.	For administration and operation of agricultural, ranch, and other non-urban properties, determine whether the bank	
		uses bank personnel to manage and administer the property.
		uses independent agents to manage and administer the property.
		ensures that the manager and administrator are qualified.
		has operating tenant agreements reviewed by bank counsel when tenant operators are engaged to operate the properties.
6.	Does the bank have procedures for verifying the amount of farm commodities, such as grain and tobacco, stored in elevators or warehouses (for example, by inspecting warehouse receipts)?	
Notes/comments:		

Appendix D

Farm and Ranch Review Worksheet

A "no" response indicates a potential weakness that warrants further investigation.

1. If a tenant farmer or rancher is used to manage the property, has the bank signed a contract with the tenant detailing the responsibilities of the tenant and the bank?

2. Does the tenant prepare a budget and operating plan?

3. Does the bank obtain or prepare financial information concerning the operations of the farm or ranch?

4. Does the bank analyze the operating results of the farm or ranch at least annually?

   - Assess the quality of the analysis:

     - Does the bank compare actual yields to expected yields?
     - Does the bank compare current yields to previous year's yields?

   - Is the farm or ranch analysis made part of the account's annual investment review?

5. Does the bank conduct periodic inspections of livestock and/or crops?

   - Assess the quality of the inspections.

6. Does the bank review expenses before payment?

7. For grain stored at grain elevators, does the bank obtain warehouse receipts?

8. For grain stored at grain elevators, does the bank review the elevator's bonding and financial condition?

9. Are inspections and appraisals current?

10. Are insurance and taxes current?

11. Are ticklers created and used?

Appendix E: Types of Life Insurance

The function of life insurance is to create a principal sum or estate, either upon the death of the insured or through the accumulation of funds set aside for investment purposes. Life insurance is most commonly used to protect a person's dependents against the undesirable financial consequences of the insured's premature death or to provide liquid assets to a person's estate.

Life insurance can be categorized into two broad types, temporary (term) and permanent insurance. While there are numerous variations of these products, most life insurance policies generally fall within either one, or a combination, of the following categories.

Term Life Insurance

Term life insurance is a contract that obligates the insurer to pay the policy's face value if the insured dies within a specified period. Term life insurance offers death benefits only and generally has no cash value or savings element. Because term life insurance provides only mortality protection, in most situations it provides the most coverage per premium dollar. While term life insurance can be relatively inexpensive for younger policyholders, term life insurance premiums generally increase with the age of the policyholder. Most term life insurance policies are renewable for certain periods or until the policyholder attains a specified age. Additionally, many term life insurance policies are convertible to permanent life insurance without the insured having to show evidence of insurability. Term life insurance is commonly used by a trust in conjunction with a home mortgage. At the death of the policyholder, the proceeds of these term life insurance policies usually are paid to a family member, rather than to the lien holder.

Permanent Life Insurance

Whole Life

The cash value of a whole life insurance policy accrues according to a guaranteed, predetermined rate of return determined by the insurance company. These policies are also referred to as "general account" products because the life insurance company's general assets support the cash value. Most policies provide lifetime protection to age 100. If the insured is still living at that age, the policy "endows," and the guaranteed cash value equals the face amount of the policy. Premiums and death benefits are guaranteed for the duration of the policy. Because premiums are constant, the cost is much higher in the early years than comparable coverage provided under a term life insurance policy. Typically, however, the cost relationship reverses in later years as the cost of term life insurance rises with the age of the insured.

Combination policies usually combine term insurance with a base whole life policy by using an attachment or rider. This combination provides for additional death benefits without a significant increase in premium cost. Please refer to the "Insurance Activities" booklet of the *Comptroller's Handbook* for further details on this and other insurance products.

Universal Life

Another permanent form of life insurance, universal life is an interest-sensitive form of life insurance, designed to provide flexibility in premium payments and death benefit protection. Policyholders can adjust the premiums, cash values, and level of protection, subject to certain limitations, over the life of the contract. Additionally, unlike whole life, the interest credited to the cash value of universal life policies is based on current interest rates, subject to an interest rate floor. Universal life has a pure insurance component (mortality protection) and a professionally managed investment component. The policyholder can pay higher premiums and maintain a high cash value. Alternatively, the policyholder can make minimal premium payments in an amount large enough to only cover mortality and other expense charges, thus not accumulating as much cash value.

Variable Life

Variable life is a form of whole life insurance. A difference between variable and traditional whole life is that the policy's cash value is invested in segregated accounts comprised of equities and other securities. Premiums may be placed in the insured's choice of stock, bond, or money market funds offered through the insurance company. The policy's death benefit and cash value of the policy depend on the underlying investment portfolio's performance, thereby shifting the investment risk to the policyholder. Generally, there is a minimum guaranteed death benefit. The policy allows for tax-deferred appreciation of the accumulated assets. Because variable life policies are classified as securities, life insurance agents selling these policies must also be registered representatives of a broker-dealer licensed by the

Financial Industry Regulatory Authority (FINRA) and must be registered with the SEC.

Variable Universal Life

Variable universal life combines the flexible premium features of universal life with the investment component of variable life. These products also are classified as securities and are subject to FINRA and SEC requirements.

Laws

12 USC 92a(h), "Loans of trust funds to officers and employees prohibited; penalties";

12USC 1464(n)(7), "Federal Savings Associations, Trust - Certain loans prohibited".

29 USC 1106, "Employee Retirement Income Security Act of 1974" (ERISA) Section 406(a)(Prohibited Transactions).

31 USC 5311 et seq., "Bank Secrecy Act."

Regulations

12 CFR 9.6(a), "Pre-Acceptance Reviews of Fiduciary Accounts."

12 CFR 9.6(b), "Initial Post-Acceptance Reviews of Fiduciary Accounts."

12 CFR 9.6(c), "Annual Investment Reviews of Fiduciary Accounts."

12 CFR 150.200, "Review of a Fiduciary Account – Must I review a prospective account before I accept it?"

12 CFR 150.210, "Review of a Fiduciary Account – Must I conduct another review of an account after I accept it?"

12 CFR 150.220, "Review of a Fiduciary Account – Are any other account reviews required?"

Comptroller's Handbook

"Agricultural Lending"

"Asset Management"

"Asset Management Operations and Controls"

"Commercial Real Estate and Construction Lending"

"Community Bank Supervision"

"Insurance Activities"

"Investment Management Services"

"Personal Fiduciary Services"

"Retirement Plan Services"

"Large Bank Supervision"

OCC Issuances

OCC Bulletin 2001-47, "Third-Party Relationships: Risk Management Principles," (November 1, 2001).

OCC Bulletin 2008-10, "Annual Reviews of Fiduciary Accounts Pursuant to 12 CFR 9.6(c)," (March 27, 2008).

OCC Bulletin 2010-42, "Interagency Appraisal and Evaluation Guidelines," (December 10, 2010).

OCC Asset Management Interpretation, Call Report Schedule RC-T – Mineral Properties (January 14, 2005).

Other References

Federal Financial Institutions Examination Council, "Bank Secrecy Act/Anti-Money Laundering Examination Manual," 2010.

IRS Revenue Ruling 59-60, "Valuing Stock of Closely Held Corporations."